The Story of Color

JOAN J. PEREZ

Balboa Press books may be ordered through booksellers or by contacting:

Balboa Press
A Division of Hay House
1663 Liberty Drive
Bloomington, IN 47403
www.balboapress.com
1 (877) 407-4847

Interior Image Credit: Olivia Hintz

ISBN: 978-1-9822-4056-1 (sc)
ISBN: 978-1-9822-4057-8 (e)

Print information available on the last page.

Balboa Press rev. date: 05/12/2020

BALBOA.PRESS
A DIVISION OF HAY HOUSE

To my son Chris who pushed, prodded, bullied
and cajoled to make my dream come true.

-Joan Perez

For all the little artists out there, who mix the
colors and make the teachers mad.

-Olivia Hintz

Once a long, long time ago when the world was very young The Wind blew all around the Earth looking for an interesting place to rest. The wind looked and looked but couldn't find that special place because everything looked the same. Nothing had color.

The Wind could not tell where the ocean ended and the sand began. Or couldn't see where the mountain met the sky.

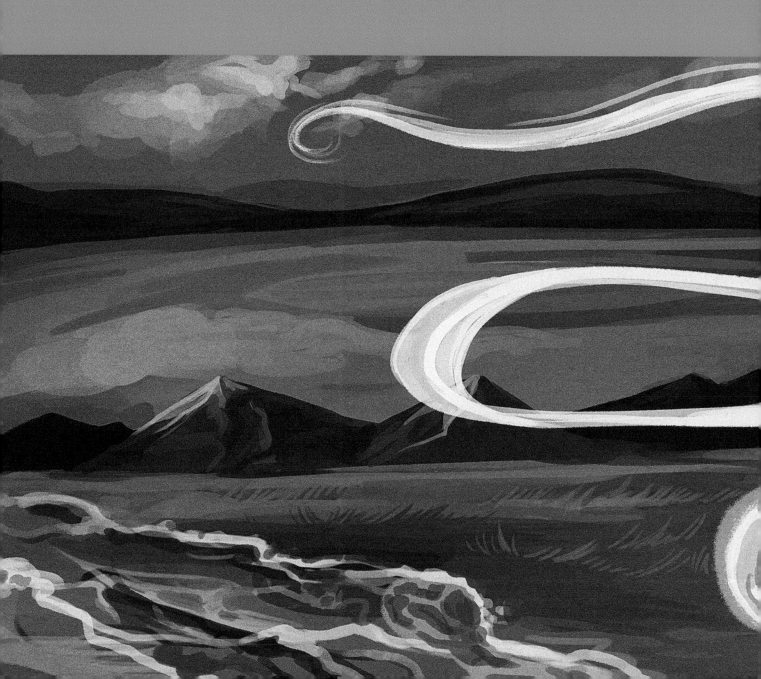

Everything looked the same and everyone looked the same too. Nothing had color.

People had no color. No one looked unique and different.

Even the animals had no color. You couldn't really see the stripes on a tiger or zebra.

Or the round spots on a leopard. Cows were sad too.

Just like the horses and zebras that looked alike, Mr. Grizzly Bear and Mr. Polar Bear looked the same too!

The Wind was feeling very sad for the Earth. So Wind decided to speak to her good friend The Rain about helping the planet look beautiful.

Team Wind and Rain decided to travel the world looking for color.

Faster and faster The Wind blew. Harder and harder The Rain fell.

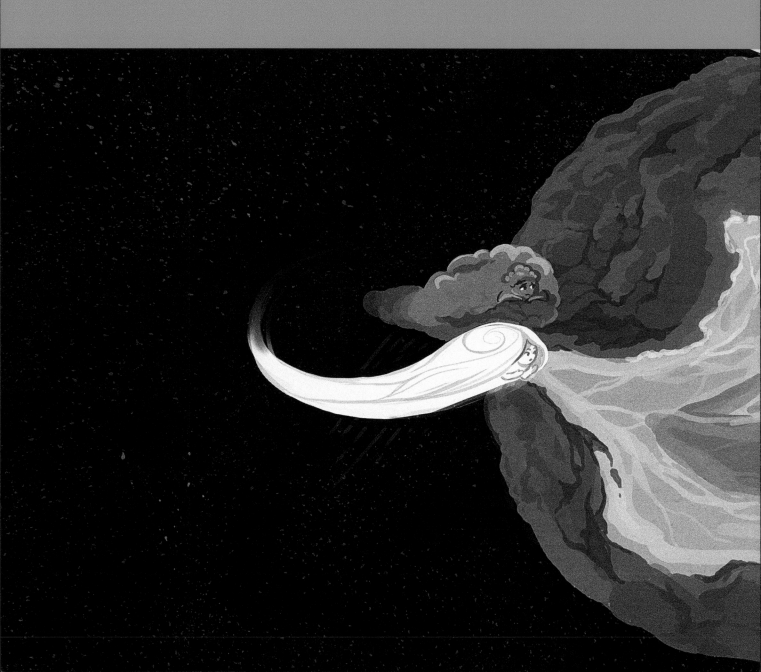

Just when they were so tired and about to give up, the sun came out and far far away they saw the first Rainbow.

The Rainbow was so huge, so tall, so grand that it circled the whole world. It had wonderful colors. There were bright yellows, and quiet blues. Happy oranges and deep reds.

There was every shade of color you can imagine. So beautiful was this Rainbow that The Wind slowed to a stop and The Rain wept gentle tears.

Bigger and bigger The Rainbow grew. Taller and taller.

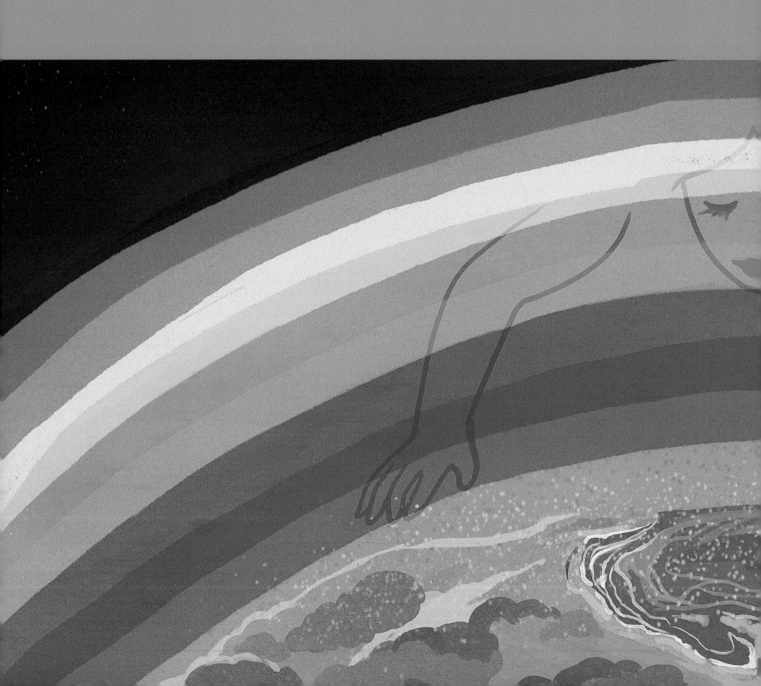

Wider and wider it got until it could not get any bigger and burst into a gazillion colored snowflakes melting softly onto the Earth and turning everything it touched into amazing color.

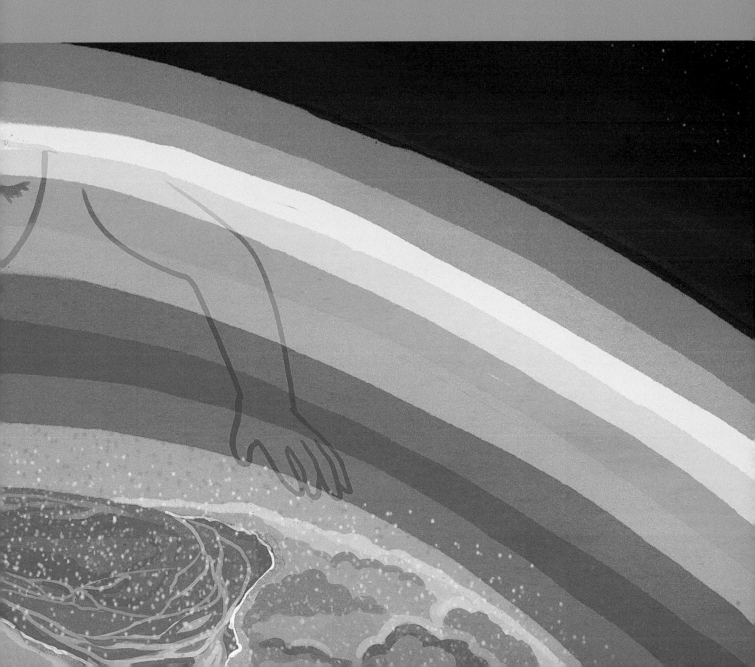

Bumblebees flew happily showing off their black and yellow bands. There were so many wonderful looking butterflies you could not name them all!

Frogs and grasshoppers jumped higher than ever happy to hide their greenness within the grass below.

Fruits and salads looked like a party on a plate. Yellow bananas, red apples were yummy-licious to look at *and* eat.

Everyone loved looking different and especially liked the jazzy colors of their clothes.

Animals from the tall giraffe to the tiny tabby cat showed off their new stripes.

The zebra looked very different from his friend the pony. Can you find all the striped creatures?

Dalmatian dog, moo cow and fierce leopard were excited too.

They knew that no other animal would have their spots in exactly the same place that they did. That made them one of a kind.

The Panda Bear looked totally different from his cousin the Brown Bear and the Polar Bear loved looking different too.

Bluebirds, Red Robins and Canaries flew between the light blue sky high up and the dark green grass below happy to show off their new bold colors.

Beautiful bugs and insects couldn't wait to show off their colorful wings and special markings as they visited gold, pink and lavender flowers.

All the people and all the animals of the world danced with joy because they were now uniquely special and one of a kind JUST LIKE YOU!

So happy was The Earth that The Wind and The Rain thanked The Rainbow for bringing color into the world and making it a more beautiful place.

And far, far away The Rainbow arched brightly to say "you're welcome".